The Theatres of Portsmouth

© 1983 John Offord

ISBN 0 903852 47 0

Phototypesetting by Inforum Ltd, Portsmouth
Printed by R J Acford, Chichester, Sussex

Published by
Milestone Publications
62 Murray Road
Horndean
Hants P08 9JL

Sponsored by
THE THEATRE ROYAL SOCIETY
New Theatre Royal
Portsmouth

Down Memory Lane I linger long,
Till evening shadows fall,
To dream of golden days bygone,
And radiant hours recall.

CURTAIN UP

THE BACKDROP

Portsmouth and Portsea, at the beginning of the 19th century, were adjacent walled-towns, whose gates closed at nights. There was an enormous military garrison; barracks, batteries, magazines and guard houses abounded. The military Governor lived in state in High Street. The sailors and Dockyard artisans tended to congregate in Portsea, but were soon to spread into Landport, Mile End and Buckland. Concurrently, the wealthy, the nobility and officers were beginning to colonize Southsea. It was these disparate groups who promoted the building of the theatres and halls in the area.

The Victorian and Edwardian eras saw the awakening of the English theatre after its long somnalence, into which it had reclined in the early 18th century. This glorious era, stimulated by Shakespeare, terminated with the dark magnificence of the Revenge Tragedies.

After the sparkling comedies of the restoration, there were no British dramatists of stature until the late 19th century, with the exceptions of Goldsmith and Sheridan.

Technically, there had been very little progress; most provincial stages were small; lit by candles and oil lamps, with primitive technical aids. The old Chichester Theatre is, externally, typical in shape and size; sadly the internal arrangements have long since disappeared.

'Theatre' was sharply divided into two types – the Music Hall and the Legitimate Theatre (Plays and Opera).

The Music Hall grew out of 'pub' entertainment, which was originally given in the bar. Later, large rooms with an end platform were built. This evolved into a full theatre building, which did not differ substantially from the legitimate theatre.

It is fascinating to conjure up a night at, say, the old South of England Music Hall in Gunwharf Road. The first theatre building was small, but some 2000 could be packed in – some at tables, others at bench-type seating, many standing or promenading. It was boisterous, uninhibited, friendly – except for the frequent brawls – brash and essentially plebian. Drink flowed; conversations went on; delicate nostrils would have been offended by the mixture of odours: the smoke, the drinks, oil and candle lamps – and the bodies! The main entertainment was the comic, and the sentimental or comic song, often with raucous participation by the patrons. Later, dramatic sketches or short plays were performed. Performance times were arranged so that soldiers could be back in the Barracks before "lights out", and citizens could enter or leave the town before the gates shut.

They were tough audiences, who could instinctively recognize talent; they could also forcibly show their disapproval – doubtless, the Gunners were to the fore when a bombardment of the stage occurred! These itinerant performers learnt their profession the hard way; there were no drama schools to help them. One can still sense the atmosphere, when a Dan Leno or a Vesta Tilley appeared; a silence would occur, and our Victorian forebears would peer through fumes, and finally roar their approval.

Prices ranged from 1d to 2/-; often with a half-price for the second half.

Scenery was very simple, and usually there were no flying facilities. Canvas drops were rolled, and perhaps a few flats may have been used. Early in the period, stage and auditoriums were lit by candles and oil lamps; limes were later introduced for spot lights and follow spots. The auditorium would have remained

illuminated during acts; it would have been impractical to 'blow out' hundreds of candles, and then re-light them for the intervals. Also the 'bouncers' could see the trouble-makers more easily! Gas lighting was introduced in the London theatres around 1815; slowly, it was introduced in the provincial theatres. This enabled more brilliant lighting to be achieved, and some very clever technical effects were produced. Above all, central control of all lighting was at last obtained. By the end of the century, electric lighting had been introduced in most theatres.

There was a continual evolution in the legitimate theatre; besides the lighting changes, there were considerable technical improvements on stage. This increasingly enabled great spectacles to be given, which involved lavish sets and elaborate visual effects. Theatres became larger, with accompanying big increases in audience capacity. There were running seats in the pit and gallery, which enabled managements to 'pack-em' in. The decor of the auditoria became progressively more ornate; exuberance, vitality – and, eventually, decadent vulgarity – prevailed.

Acting styles changed from the mannerist rhetorical form of Macready to the more naturalistic ideas of Irving, Ellen Terry and the other late Victorians. These changes were relative to the era, and, to our ears, the recorded voices of Bernhardt, Irving, Duse and the others seem stylised. In their time, they were the exciting innovators.

Theatre audiences were normally more restrained than their Music Hall colleagues; perhaps the monocled gentlemen and lorgnetted ladies in the boxes helped, by their glares, to keep their inferiors in order. Social divisions in the theatre were quite clear:-

Lower Lower Class	– exiled to the Gods, some 60 feet up drab, painted brick, staircases; the entrance was usually at the rear or sides of the theatre. There were running hard benches, with no backrests – except the knees of the person behind! Toilets and the bar were functional. But then they only paid 6d, and half price at 9 pm.
Upper Lower Classes	– for 1/-, they would go to the pit, which had upholstered running benches, but fitted with a back rest. Toilets and bar were recognisable.
Lower Middle Classes	– for 2/-, they would clamber up some 40 feet of staircase, but it had a wooden handrail and plastered walls. They sat on plush tip-up seats; the bar was quite attractive, and the toilets were almost civilized.
Upper Middle Class	– Together with the upper class, they were privileged to alight from their carriages by the porte-cochère, and mount the Grand Staircase to take their place in the commodious armchairs in the Dress Circle. Later, there would also have been the orchestra stalls. Evening dress was derigueur. There would be an opulent rococo bar for gentlemen, and marble loos! All for 4/-.
Upper Class	– For 1 or 2 guineas they had the splendid isolation of a box. Hopefully, they had a superb view of the stage, and were also superbly seen themselves.

As Mrs. Alexander might well have written:

The rich man in his box
The poor man at the top,
God made them, high or lowly,
and thus, each knew his lot.

Managements became progressively concerned with morality, at least publicly. A typical programme notice declares:

"SPECIAL NOTICE It being the desire of the Manager that the entertainment offered at this Theatre shall be at all times absolutely free from objectionable features; the co-operation of the Public is invited to this end. Anyone giving information of any suggestive or offensive word or action upon the Stage that may have escaped the notice of the management will greatly oblige. Any incivility from Employees please report to Manager." (Hippodrome Programme of 1907)

Yes, times have changed.

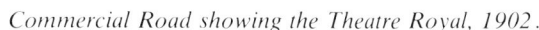

Commercial Road showing the Theatre Royal, 1902.

THE THEATRES OF PORTSMOUTH 1840 - 1914

At the start of this period, there was only one regular theatre: the old Theatre Royal in High Street, just north of Buckingham House, on a site now occupied by part of the Grammar School (originally the Clarence Barracks). During this period, incredible though it may appear today, ten theatres were built in Portsmouth. In addition, the King's Theatre, Portland Hall and South Parade Pier Theatre were built in Southsea. They were, in chronological order of first building:-

1. Theatre Royal, High Street.

Built 1761?
Demolished 1856

2. Grecian Saloon, later Landport Theatre, Mary-le-Bon Street, Landport.

Built 1843
Closed 1850

3. South of England Music Hall, later Barnard's Royal Amphitheatre, Gunwharf Road.

Built 1856
Enlarged and rebuilt at various times
Destroyed by fire 1890

4. Theatre Royal, Landport.
Previous building on site converted to a theatre 1856.

Rebuilt 1884
Enlarged 1900

5. Royal Albert Theatre, later the Prince's Theatre, Lake Road.

Built 1868
Destroyed by fire 1882
Rebuilt 1891
Destroyed by bombs 1940

6. St. George's Hall and Opera House, Ordnance Row.

Period of use 1860s to 1870s

7. Ginnett's New Hippodrome, adjacent to Town Station.	Built 1881 (as a circus) Closed 1892
8. People's Palace of Varieties, later Vento's, Lake Road.	Built 1884 Demolished 1980
9. The Empire, later the Coliseum, Edinburgh Road.	Built 1891 Demolished 1958
10. The Hippodrome, Commercial Road.	Built 1907 Destroyed by bombing 1941

Other halls were occasionally used for theatrical purposes and three huge magnificent theatres were planned, but never materialized.

However, the Theatre Royal outshone all its rivals, and became one of the loveliest theatres in England, presenting the greatest actors, actresses, operas, musicals and plays of the period. It owed its fame to one man, its creator – John Walters Boughton, who named it "The Premier Theatre in the south of England". He rebuilt it twice, rebuilt the Prince's Theatre, and built the King's Theatre.

The theatres prospered in this period; managers vied with each other; improvements in one theatre caused frantic improvements to be carried out in the others. To some extent, the various theatres catered for distinctive audiences. The South of England Music Hall was the main venue for the Army and Navy, Vento's for the great artisan areas of Landport, Stamshaw and Buckland. Except for the Theatre Royal and Princes, they were all music halls or variety theatres. The Hippodrome occasionally presented opera and plays.

Finally, there were theatres at various times, and in various places, in Gosport. Noel Coward made his first stage appearance, as a boy, at Lee-on-Solent pier.

It has proved very difficult to obtain much information about some of the smaller halls; often they only survived a few years. *The Portsmouth Times* (1850–1926), an excellent paper, provided an enormous amount of information; likewise *The Era* – a national magazine.

Theatre Royal, High Street, Portsmouth

The origins are clouded, but it would seem most likely that the last theatre on that site was built in 1761. It survived until 1854, when the War Office acquired the land; the building was demolished in 1856, together with all the Georgian houses up to what is now called Cambridge Circus. The Clarence Barracks, now the Grammar School, were constructed on the site.

Its last few years were pathetic, often it only played one night each week. On such occasions, the management arranged a spe-

Theatre Royal, High Street, Portsmouth. A drawing of the theatre in 1853 just prior to its demolition. By a pencilled inscription, it would seem that Owen had bought the theatre for £3,300. It is the same Owen who had built so many of the fine villas in Southsea. Portsmouth City Archivist.

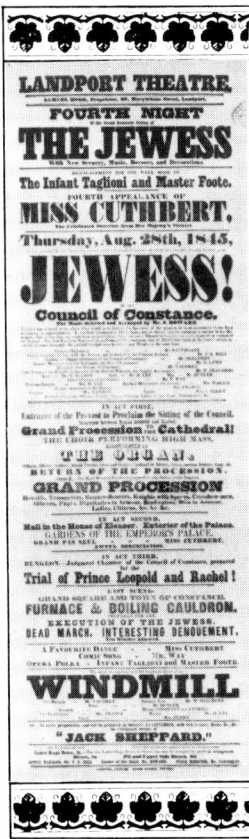

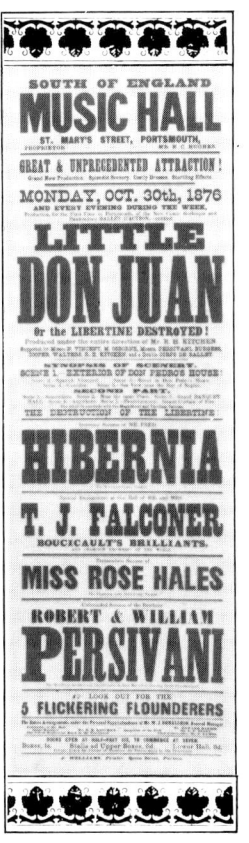

Left: Landport Theatre (formerly Grecian Saloon) poster of 1845. It was in Mary-le-Bon Street, not far from the Central Library. Right: South of England Music Hall – St Mary's Street & Gunwharf Road. Poster of 1867. Evolved out of the old 'Blew Bell' Inn, it had various names, and was eventually destroyed by fire in 1890.

cial crossing of the new-fangled Floating Bridge to Gosport for the benefit of Gosportonians, after the evening performance. Children from the Town Charity Schools were allowed in free to some matinee performances, but only if 'attended by a teacher'. Poor teachers – mutatis mutandis!

A poster of 1849 announced it had been converted into a "Magnificent Amphitheatre; Pyramids on 3 horses". The "Art of Riding and properly managing the horse daily at the Amphitheatre" was announced in another poster of the same year.

Thus, slowly a famed theatre died, and for a few years there was no permanent dramatic or lyrical theatre in the town.

The Grecian Saloon – later The Landport Theatre, 20 Mary-le-Bon Street

The theatre opened in March 1843, under the direction of Mr. T. E. Ball. The licence was only granted provided the pawnbroker business was removed from the premises; it would have been an interesting combination! The actual site of this theatre could not have been very far from the present Central Library Theatre. Mary-le-Bone Street was off Greatham Street.

William Shalders, who had been a popular actor and Stage Manager at the High Street Theatre, repeated these roles at the Grecian Saloon. From extant posters, it seems initially to have presented variety, with accent on music and dancing. It also presented 'DISSOLVING VIEWS' – using an 'Oxy-hydrogen lime light'; a very early instance of combining 'pictures' and stage shows. Views shown included:- 'The Chase', 'The Capture', 'Nelson', 'The Queen and Prince Albert', all accompanied by suitable music, played by the band. Boxes were 1/-, pit 6d – both included refreshments; stalls cost 6d, but apparently did not have the privilege of refreshments. Total accommodation was about 700.

By 1845, it had been renamed the Landport Theatre. (Not to be confused with the Landport Hall, which subsequently became the Theatre Royal). A Samuel Hogg took control of the theatre around this time, and he mainly presented straight plays, some of which were shared with the High Street Theatre. Many of these productions were evidently quite spectacular. In August 1845, a 'Melodramatic Spectacle' called 'The Jewess' or 'The Council of Constance' was presented. Included was a performance of High Mass sung by a full choir! As usual in this period, a 'laughable' farce was often given after a serious drama. A poster of 1846 advertises a drama 'Lucille', followed by 'The Windmill', a comic piece. The evidently superior productions caused an increase of price – boxes were now 2/- – a 100% increase.

In 1850, Hogg went bankrupt, and that was the end of this theatre. Hogg stated at the time that it cost him £50 per week to operate the theatre, and that initially he had to make an outlay of £1150.

The South Of England Music Hall

This theatre had its origins in the Blue-Bell (formerly Blew Bell) Inn in St. Mary's Street, near the old church of the same dedication. The Power Station, in its turn now demolished, occupied the site of theatre and church.

Like many of the old inns, it possessed a music room, used mainly for 'sing-songs'. By 1854, when a William Brown took over the licence, there was no theatre left in Portsmouth. He therefore, decided to build a small music hall, in association with the inn. This was opened in 1856, just before the Theatre Royal, its clientelle being chiefly soldiers, sailors and their womenfolk. It had a somewhat unsavoury reputation, and brawls were common. A poster of 8th March 1858 announced a wide variety of acts – a comic occulist, the theatre's own dancers in quadrilles and waltzes, 'niggers' from the south and pantominists. Doors opened at 5 pm and the start was at 5.30 pm. "Strict attention would be paid to Garrison Times". It also stated that wines, spirits etc. of the finest quality were available, a pleasure the soldiers no doubt enjoyed in great quantity!

By 1860, business was so good that Brown decided to enlarge the theatre. The new building was erected over the old hall, and, astonishingly, there was only a two day break between the closing of the old hall, and the opening of the new. (They worked in those days!). It opened on 20th August, and accommodated 2000 patrons – at that time it was the largest theatre in town. *The Portsmouth Times* reported, "It had been designed and built by Mr. H. Lawrence and for architectural effect and acoustic properties is unsurpassed in the provinces. Whilst ventilation and accommodation of visitors have received special attention. The chaste and elegant decorations were designed by C. B. Wilson. The Hall is illuminated with numerous glass chandeliers, and there are 16 fires in the Hall."

It attracted many famous names, and the performances were presided over by a chairman. Patrons were issued with tokens, worth 1½p, for which they could obtain two pints of beer! Perhaps they were 'the good old days'.

In 1872, the theatre was redecorated and reseated; limelights were used for the stage, It had it's own scenic artist, and an orchestra of nine; T. W. Boughton, later of the Royal, was the flutist. There were two 'grand saloons' for the box tier, and a number of 'stage reserved seats'.

At this time the prices were:-

Private boxes	2/-
Boxes	1/-
Stalls, upper side boxes	6d
Lower Hall	3d

New regulations were also published at this time; they included:-

(1) Ladies will not be admitted unless with a gentleman.
(2) Ladies leaving the hall will not be re-admitted the same evening.
(3) Gentlemen only to be served with refreshments!

Allsopps Pale Ale and Guinness draught or bottled – seemed the favoured drink for the gentlemen.

In 1873, Brown retired and sold the hall to the London Alhambra Company, who subsequently renamed it as the Alhambra Music Hall. In 1878, the theatre was burnt down, a fate which attended most theatres. The average life of a theatre was under twenty years at that time, which is understandable, when the type of lighting and heating employed is considered. Within a year it was rebuilt, and renamed the New (South of England) Grand Palace. Its capacity was 3000; it included orchestra stalls, pit, a tier of boxes and a gallery. Famous names still walked the boards there, including Marie Lloyd, who was "deservedly encored for dancing". She had to share her visit with twelve arabs, who topped the bill!

In 1885, a Mr. Barnard, from the Palace of Varieties, Chatham, took over the theatre, and it was renamed, yet again, as Barnard's Royal Amphitheatre. According to records, it did not do so well; there was more competition in the town. It finally succumbed to another fire in 1890; it was curtains, for this time it was not rebuilt.

Interestingly, the licence was transferred to the new Empire Theatre in Edinburgh Road; thus, in a way, the old music hall kept the tradition going from the time of the Blue-bell Inn, until the Empire was eventually demolished in 1958.

The Saint George's Hall And Opera House

This theatre is first mentioned in May 1868, and was situated near St, George's Church in Ordnance Row. It was evidently a somewhat pedestrian place, and possessed only a single 'gallery'. However, it did live up to its title and presented some opera. Various posters proclaimed Miss Laura Pyne's Comic Opera Company, which presented "Poor as a Rat" by Summer and Offenbach's "The Treasure found by the Lamp Light".

An advert in the paper on 18 June 1871 announced that "the continual success, great excitement and crowded and delightful audiences" demanded an extension of the current show. It went on to say that "for the third, and positively last, week, in the golden palace of enchantment, and theatre of mirth and variety, there would be pantomime and a musical clairvoyant." They wanted each evening 1000 ladies and gentlemen to be mesmerised. It must have been an interesting sight! Very little more about this grand sounding theatre has been discovered; perhaps it was "mesmerised" into some other use. Seats cost 2/-, 1/- and 6d. A Mr. G. A. Atkins was the proprietor, and lived near-by.

Ginnett's New Hippodrome

This was in Commercial Road, adjacent to the Town Station, and started as a circus in 1881. It was rebuilt, redecorated a number of times; also it went under various names. It never appeared to achieve any stability, in spite of its interesting arrangements!

An advert in the paper January 1884 stated "Mr. Ginnett's New Year's Treat to the old on Wednesday afternoon, January 9th 1884, when all poor men and women will be admitted free to the circus and regaled with tea and cake. They must be over 70. All those over 90 will receive in addition to the above the sum of 5/- and those over 100 receive £1". Considering the period, and

Circus Royal – Commercial Road. Later also known as Ginnett's Hippodrome.

13

the age qualifications, most likely the munificence did not cost him a great deal!

In March of 1884, it was revamped, and called "The New Pavillion and Grand Palace of Variety" – long names were in vogue. It possessed a musical director (Charles Bayman) and a resident scenic artist (G. B. Wilson). The old circus ring had been floored and carpeted, and fitted with fauteuils. Ginnet still owned the place, and circus acts continued to be a feature. It was not successful, and by May of the same year, the building was up to let.

In 1888, it was being used for boxing, and a famed pugilist, Mr. J. L. Sullivan, threw a challenge to the men of Portsmouth, and offered a handsome prize if they should beat him.

Another rebuilding occurred in 1889; it re-opened on 23 December as "The new Alhambra Music Hall", under the direction of Fred Fordham.

The gallery had been converted into a grand promenade, which was extended right round the building, a total length of 300 feet. The paper reported "cosy retiring rooms and well furnished private boxes" (all very interesting!). In front of the orchestra were fauteuils, whilst small tables and chairs were all around. It held 5000 people – an enormous number. Its musical director, H. E. Ferguson, was billed as coming from the Eden Theatre in Paris.

It was still not successful, and it finally closed on 6th June 1892. Quite likely the opening of the Empire and the Princes Theatres in the previous year affected business. They were grand theatres, designed by two of the most famous architects of the day – Phipps and Matcham respectively. Fred Fordham later re-appeared as a 'turn' in the St. James' Hall, Charlotte Street, which was chiefly a cinematograph hall.

Vento's Temple Of Varieties

It was first built in 1884, by Frank Pearce, and located in Lake Road on the corner with Leonard Street, just beyond the then ruined site of the Prince's Theatre. In 1886, Harry Vento took the lease, hence its title.

It was basically a music hall, with an orchestra of five. There were no flying facilities, and the stage curtain 'rolled-up', quite a common method in small halls. For each act, a bell would be rung, and the Stage Manager appeared from the wings with a panel, which announced the act, and placed it on an easel. It was evidently a friendly, informal place; exchanges between artists and public were welcomed. Patrons were allowed to bring fish and chips, oranges and nuts into the auditorium; and no doubt, on occasions, the artists were the unwilling recipients of such viands. Definitely it must have been a 'matey' place.

No alcohol was sold on the premises.

Seat costs were:-

Boxes	1/-
Orchestra Stalls	6d
Balcony	4d
Pit	3d
Galley	2d

In 1891, there occurred a very amusing legal case between Vento, the lessee, and the owner, Pearce.

The Portsmouth Times headlined on the 10th December 1891:- "Vento defaults on five week's rent to Mr. Pearce".

The contretemps was caused, when the licencing authority considered they were unable to renew the licence owing to the Theatre's condition. According to the Portsmouth Times of 24 October 1891, "the interior was in a very poor state, filth had accumulated everywhere, and a piece of canvas was put over a hole in the roof, near a naked light". In defence, Vento protested

Peoples' Palace of Varieties (formerly Vento's), Lake Road, Portsmouth, 1884. A music hall until 1910, when it became a cinema. Demolished in 1980.

that the rent was only payable, under the terms of the lease, if the building was in a fit state to be used as a music hall.

The comic element in court was introduced by a witness, a bricklayer, called Moore. When questioned about the 'hole' in the roof, he explained that he was sent to Vento's, and by the instructions of both Vento and Pearce he went onto the roof, and there made some holes in it, with a 4 lb. hammer!

Defence Counsel: "But did Mr. Pearce tell you to do that?"

Moore: "I can't remember if anyone told me".

Defence: "Do you mean to tell us, that you went on the roof, and wantonly nailed holes into it?"

Moore: "Yes" – Laughter.

Defence: "Do you really tell us that?"

Moore: "That's right". More laughter.

Defence: "What was the object of the canvas over the hole in the roof?"

Moore: "I think it was put there to let the air in – or out". Loud laughter.

Vento lost the case, and Pearce took over running the Theatre directly. Pearce had the theatre repaired, and completely redecorated. Alas, on the day it was due to re-open, it was destroyed by fire. There is a story that his hair turned white overnight; understandably as he had sunk all his money into the venture. In good tradition, the show went on – on some nearby waste ground. The public rallied round him, and helped him to rebuild his theatre. In a modest fashion, it prospered – many of the leading music hall stars appeared there, including Hetty King, Vesta Tilley (later Lady de Frece) and the Leno family.

The total capacity was probably around 700. The stage must have been small, and technical facilities minimal, but it apparently engineered a faithful patronage and earnt an affection.

By 1910 it had become a cinema, and later renamed the Palladium. By the second war it had closed, and lay derelict until it became a store, first for Bolloms, and finally for Blundells. The sad-looking shell, once so vibrant with music, singing and laughter, was demolished in 1980.

Minor Halls And Theatres

In addition to the major theatres, there were a number of halls and theatres, often used for many other purposes, which had relatively short lives. Sadly, for all the theatres of this period, there are only sketches and photographs of a few, and one can only imagine them from old cuttings in the papers, and from details given on posters.

Queen's Rooms, Lion Terrace

This hall must have been one of the most fascinating. Great scenic pageants were presented – with the use of rolling scenery. One poster announces that 6500 feet of transparent scenery would be used, and that some views were 40 feet across. They were wound across the stage, with dramatic lighting and sound effects.

In August 1885, the "Crimean War" was presented; scenes given included "The Charge of the Light Brigade", "Views of the Bosphorous", "The Battle of Alma" etc., all painted by the drawing master to the Prince of Wales. The paintings commenced to move at 8 o'clock precisely.

First class seats were 2/-, second class 1/- and back or promenade 6d.

Another poster proclaimed that "Napoleon crossing the Alps" would be shown.

Music hall was also presented; magicians appeared to be a favourite turn, and were frequently billed. Lectures were given; in

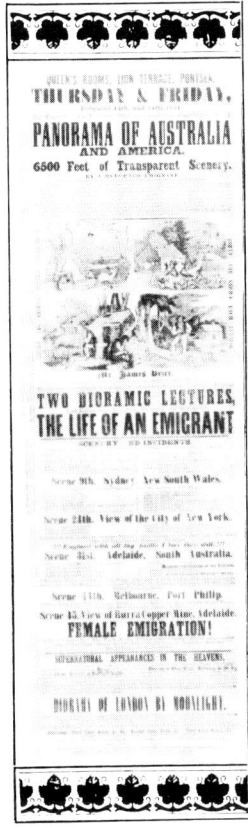

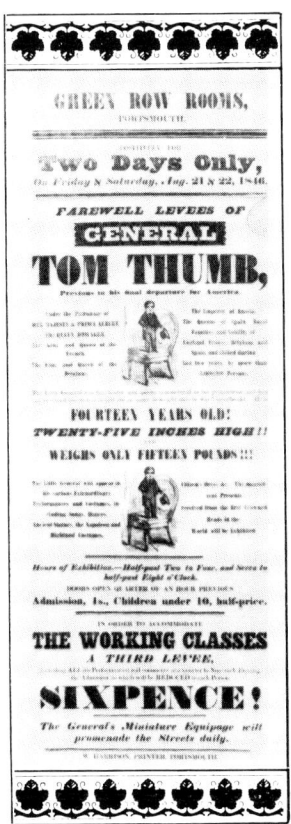

Left: Queen's Rooms, Lion Terrace. A poster of 1851. Frequently presented great panorama shows, as well as music hall and lectures.
Right: Green Row Rooms – a poster of 1846.

April 1849 a talk was given on "The electric light – superior even to the Sun"!

Batty's Royal Arena

It was situated in King's Street, Southsea, and appears to have been mainly a circus. Posters proclaim that "The Circus will be brilliantly lit with gas, and every care taken to add to the comfort of the visitor". It was a touring date, and whole productions from London Theatres were seen there. On occasions, the Mayor was a distinguished patron.

Boxes were 2/-, pit 1/- and the gallery 6d.

Royal Britannia Theatre

Another music hall at 292/4 Commercial Road. It had an orchestra of six, whilst wines and refreshments of "the highest quality" were offered to the public. A poster of 1867 announced trapezists, ventriloquists, clowns and a comic ballet, performed by the whole cast.

Private boxes were 1/-, boxes 6d, stalls 4d and the lower hall 3d.

No boys were admitted unless accompanied by parents or friends. It would be interesting to learn, what had prompted this ban.

Crown Assembly Rooms

Located in Pembroke Road; it appeared to favour magicians. A poster of 1842 announced the appearance of "The Great Wizard". Included in the programme were "Transformation and Cabalistic Conjurations", "Peruvian Sacrifice with the mysteries of Vesta, Goddess of Fire" and "The Wonderful Gun Delusion". Sounds a good night out!

It was also stated that "The Wizard begs to inform the nobility, gentry and amateurs he has got up a few sets of magnificent apparatus for performances of parlour magic, in which he will make any gentleman perfect in two hours. The set (7 tricks), 5 guineas; single trick 1 guinea." At those prices, it certainly must have been a game for the gentry alone! Prices were:- Front circle 2/-, back circle 1/- and gallery 6d.

The Empire Theatre

The Portsmouth Empire Palace Company, composed in the main of local business men, commissioned C.J. Phipps to design the theatre, and Cooke of Fratton to construct it.

The grand opening was on the 2nd November 1891; some idea of the interior can be gained from a photograph taken in the 1950s.

The Portsmouth Times gave a detailed account of the theatre. Great attention had been paid to safety, especially from fire. Phipps must have been especially conscious of this hazard, for his Exeter Theatre Royal had been destroyed by fire, shortly after its opening in 1886, with considerable loss of life. The Court had levelled serious criticisms at his design.

The Empire, built of brick, had two cantilevered tiers with an iron framework and concrete flooring. A massive wall, with an iron-framed safety curtain, separated stage and auditorium. These precautions are now statutory, but were not so in the past.

The Empire marked an evolution in music-hall design, which previously had been completely different from that of the legitimite theatre. As mentioned earlier they often originated in a Tavern, like the South of England Music Hall, and were merely a large room or hall, sometimes with a small balcony. By the late 19th century, all that was changing, and the new music-halls, or variety theatres as they were becoming known, resembled more and more the straight drama houses. The stage might be smaller,

The Empire Theatre, Edinburgh Road. An early photograph. The owners wanted to build a much larger theatre in Stanhope Road in 1900. Opposition to its erection was led by Boughton of the Royal.

with fewer technical facilities, and the decor perhaps relatively a little 'vulgar'!

It is interesting to observe how the wheel of Music Hall has turned full circle; it developed as a 'pub' entertainment, and evolved into Variety played in Grands and Empires. They, in their turn, have disappeared, and 'variety' has returned to taverns and, especially in the north, to Clubs.

It was a sign of these changes, that the Company managed to secure Phipps as their architect, for he was more accustomed to design the grand, beautiful opera houses, than small music halls.

The ground floor had comfortable seats with armrests, whilst the balcony (first tier) had most luxurious seats, upholstered in blue figured plush velvet. On audience right, there was a large promenade and saloon, an echo of the old music-hall. Two boxes separated the balcony each side from the proscenium arch. Together with the gallery (second tier), the theatre could seat 800, with another 200 standing.

It was a square-shaped auditorium, with a prevailing colour scheme of blue-grey, ivory and gold leaf. (All theatres seemed to have been able to adorn their theatres with libraries of gold leaf; sadly 'gold' paint has to suffice nowadays). The panels of the tiers were originally adorned with mythological figures, whilst the ceiling had an elaborate rococo pattern, spraying out from the centre sunlight. Initially, the auditorium was lit by gas, the mantles being enclosed by opal shades. The sunlight, a multiple jet gas burner, gave both illumination, and with a flue above it, helped to extract the obnoxious fumes (and other pungent odours!) which plagued gas lit theatres. Trapeze fittings were permanently attached to the ceiling, and wire supporting ropes could be attached to the gallery. Phipps must have winced at such plebian disfigurement to his carefully designed auditorium!

Patronage must have been drawn from that of the old Halls, such as the South of England, Ginnet's Hippodrome and others

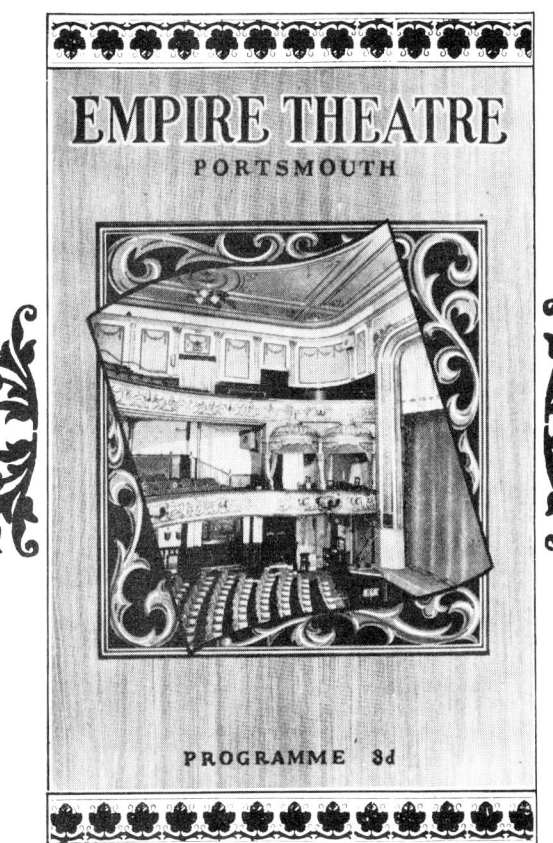

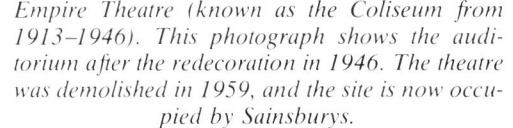

Empire Theatre (known as the Coliseum from 1913–1946). This photograph shows the auditorium after the redecoration in 1946. The theatre was demolished in 1959, and the site is now occupied by Sainsburys.

which were no more. Seats cost more, but were considerably cheaper than those at the Royal or Princes. Private boxes were 1 guinea and half a guinea, balcony 2/-, hall (i.e. ground floor) 1/- and the gallery 6d.

In 1900, the Empire Palace Company planned to build a new super theatre on the west side of Stanhope Road, on the site of the present Zurich building. It was to have a frontage of 200 feet, and a depth of 80 feet, with three tiers. The magistrates refused a licence for the projected theatre, and the plan was dropped. However, in 1913 the old theatre was completely renovated, and renamed the Coliseum. Evidently, the management were feeling increased competition from the Hippodrome and Kings Theatre, both new and splendid theatres, and both presenting variety at this time.

The Portsmouth Times reported that the auditorium was redecorated, and the plaster highlights picked out in real English gold leaf. Two boxes were added each side of the gallery and three rows of fauteuils introduced in front of the stalls. The entrance foyer and staircases received embellishments of ornamental plaster work, and hand-painted figures adorned the panels. Commissionaires, in magnificent new uniforms, and "a waiting staff of daintily attired waiting maids" greeted patrons.

Marie Lloyd topped the bill at the gala re-opening. Whilst such stars were not always on the bill, a wide variety of popular acts were presented, and the theatre prospered. In the 1930s, a Christmas pantomime became a regular event; they were very traditional, with plenty of 'custard-pie' action! In 1933, there was a resident repertory company doing twice nightly shows; this venture only lasted a few weeks, and was not repeated.

In 1941, its old rival, the Hippodrome, was destroyed, and the Kings had gone over to straight theatre. After the War, the theatre was again re-decorated, re-seated, re-curtained and the gallery side boxes were removed. Perhaps this was to answer competition from the Royal, which became a variety theatre in 1948. Once more, it reverted to its original name, the Empire, and it became the cleanest and most comfortable theatre in the city. For a few years it flourished, until by the mid 1950s, when television invaded the south, and there were fewer and fewer good acts on the road. Even the "We never clothe 'em" shows failed to draw audiences. It had a few moments of strange, final, partial glory, when the Portsmouth Grand Opera Company presented 'Faust' and 'Die Fledermaus' in 1957 and 1958.

The end came in September 1958, when it was sold and demolished, and a supermarket was erected on the site. It was tragic that a fine Victorian Theatre, designed by one of the best theatre architects, should have been destroyed. Its size, facilities and location would have made it an ideal venue for many cultural purposes, which have hitherto lacked a base in the city.

It was said that the licensee tried to lease the Theatre Royal, which at that time was closed.

Technical Data

Stage depth	21 feet
Proscenium Opening	28 feet
Width of Auditorium	56 feet
Depth of Auditorium	54 feet
Two tiers – balcony and gallery	
All the bars and saloons were on audience right	

The Hippodrome

This was the eighteenth theatre built, and owned, by Sir Walter de Frece, most of which bore the name 'Hippodrome', although technically none of them were a 'hippodrome'. (The London Hippodrome was an exception, and its ground floor could be used

Hippodrome – Commercial Road – facade.

for equestrian spectacles, and even flooded for aquatic scenes!).

It was completed in 1907 on a site previously occupied by two houses, surrounded by large gardens. The theatre was designed by Bertie Crewe, a celebrated Edwardian theatre architect, and was typical of music-hall design of that period. It was located on the opposite side of the road to the Theatre Royal, and a little towards the Town Hall. One can still walk down the stalls floor towards the stage area, over 40 years after it was destroyed; looking up at the north wall, silhouettes of the tiers can still be seen.

The theatre cost de Frece £40,000 to build and equip, an enormous sum in 1907. The auditorium was magnificent, decorated in white and gold, with deep crimson curtaining and seating. There were two tiers – the grand tier and gallery; four boxes flanked either side of the Derbyshire marble proscenium arch. Generous spacing was allowed between the rows in the stalls, so that late comers could pass along without disturbing those already seated. (Theatre designers might note this point carefully!) There were five large saloons, but initially no alcohol was served; however, 'dainty teas' were available at matinees!

Backstage was very cramped, the stage itself was only 30 feet deep. Music halls, of course, did not require the space or technical facilities required by a dramatic and lyrical theatre, such as the Royal. Eight dressing rooms were slotted into various odd spaces; number 7 and 8 were below stage – their occupants must have been well down the Bill!

Marie Tempest performed the opening ceremony. Her arrival at the Station, and the carriage drive to the Theatre was filmed, and shown at the Gala Opening. It would be splendid if this precious archive were ever discovered in some dusty corner. The opening was before an invited audience of 1000; Bertie Crewe and Vesta Tilley, now Lady de Frece, were amongst the distinguished audience.

It was a typical music hall programme; included were:-

Hippodrome – boxes and tiers.

Hippodrome – proscenium crown.

Hippodrome – the auditorium ceiling.

Hippodrome – a saloon – where "Dainty Teas" were served.

Mr. Jam Rudenyi – the celebrated Hungarian violinist
Mr. Henry Moore – a 'mimic'
Alburtas and Miller – 'jugglers'
Madame Alice Esty, supported by a full operatic chorus in the
    'Miserere' scene from 'Il Trovatore'
The Hippodrome Bioscope

This last was a regular feature in the early years. There were often 'cinematinées' during this period.

All the leading music-hall artists appeared in the theatre; such names included were:-

Vesta Tilley (Lady de Frece)
Marie Lloyd
Nellie Wallace
George Robey, who had shares in the Theatre Royal Company
Harry Randall
Little Titch
Gracie Fields
Elsie and Doris Walters, and so many others

The Hippodrome was considered more 'high class' than the old Empire; it was 'nice', and one could take the children there! This was, perhaps, an unfair comparison with the older theatre.

From April 1933, 'NON-STOP VARIETY, REVUE AND FILMS' were presented; the complete programme lasted three hours, one hour only being films. It claimed to provide "The biggest entertainment in the south of England, at the cheapest prices". Evening prices were:- Stalls 2/- and 1/3, Grand Circle 1/6 and 1/-, pit 9d and gallery 6d.

This was a very difficult period for theatre; 'talkies' had just arrived; the cinema boom was on. The Prince's Theatre had shown films since 1924, the Kings Theatre gave its first 'talkies' in 1931, and the Royal in 1932.

The Hippodrome experiment did not last long and, later the

Hippodrome – Vesta Tilley (Lady de Frece). She frequently played at Vento's Palace of Varieties, and later at the Hippodrome.

same year, it reverted to variety during the week, and a full film programme on Sundays only.

Occasionally, an opera or a play was presented; pantomimes were also introduced. 'Peter Pan', complete with flying, was presented on one occasion.

The theatre was destroyed in the great Blitz of 10th January 1941. When some of the remaining walls were demolished with explosives, all the windows in the façade of the Royal were also 'demolished'.

One stone-faced fragment of an end wall remains, it would be very fitting for this sole relic to be incorporated in the building, eventually erected on this long-deserted site. Perhaps a plaque recalling the old theatre could be affixed. It should be.

Technical Data
Seating (1907)

Stalls	465	Pit 280
Grand Circle	352	
Gallery	624	
8 Boxes	52	
Standing	100	
TOTAL	1873	

There were 9 exits, and it was calculated that a full house could be evacuated in three minutes.

Stage Depth	30 feet
Proscenium Opening	31 feet
10 Dressing rooms, including two below stage	
Width of theatre	64 feet
Depth of auditorium	64 feet

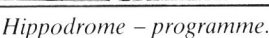

Hippodrome – programme.

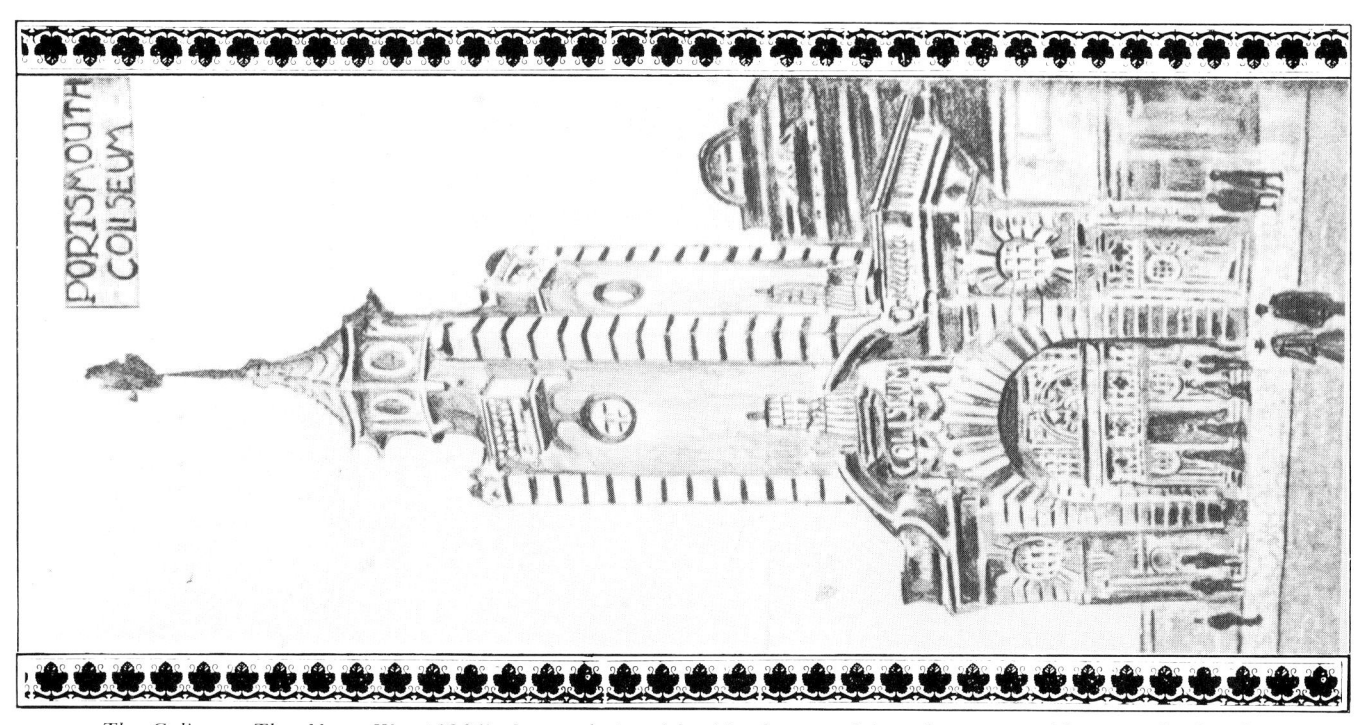

The Coliseum That-Never-Was (1906). It was designed by Matcham, and bore heavy resemblance to the London Coliseum. It was to have been built in Greatham Street. Boughton, of the Royal, led the opposition to its building.

28

The Coliseum

This was the colossal, that never was! The Portsmouth Empire Palace Company, (owner of the Empire, renamed Coliseum in 1913) had no connection whatever with the venture. It was the brainchild of a new company, called the Portsmouth Coliseum Syndicate, who in 1906, bought a huge site in Greatham Street, bounded on the sides by Swan Street and Marylebone Street. This latter street was the site of the old Grecian Saloon. Frank Matcham, designer of the London Coliseum, drew up plans for this 'super' theatre. The frontage was 116 feet, the depth of the site 225 feet and the stage would have had a depth of 90 feet. The ground area was double that of the Theatre Royal. A colossal tower, complete with an observation room and 'dizzily-perched' balconies, would have dominated this huge theatre, and the whole area.

There was to be seating for 3000, with space for 1000 standing; it was calculated, that with 15 exits, this vast audience could be cleared in three minutes. Enormous palatial waiting rooms, hung with oriental draperies and furnished with armchairs, would provide a waiting area for the second house. Stalls patrons would proceed via a special subway, planned to run under a raised pit. Matcham pointed out that this would not only offer pit customers a better view, but "at the same time, it secures the privacy of the stalls by making the division between the two more decided". (Also, it would have meant that unscrupulous pit customers would not have been able to sneak into vacant stalls seats, when the house lights were lowered!). At the rear of the pit, there was to have been a raised promenade.

The Corporation approved of the plans, but when application for a licence was made, immediately there was opposition. This was led by the Chief Constable, the Portsmouth Hippodrome Company (understandably!) and the Citizens' Union. The promoters countered this by a petition signed by 116 residents of the area, who favoured the scheme. This had a reverse effect, for the Chief Constable 'spied' that a "number of loose women" had signed the petition, no doubt hoping for increased trade from the 'toppers', patronizing the theatre.

The magistrates, although they declared themselves "favourably impressed" by the scheme, threw out the application. In effect, they said, "Get your theatre built, and then we will see about a licence."

The grand design never materialized; perhaps after the action of the magistrates, the necessary finance was not forthcoming.

Its erection would certainly have changed the Portsmouth theatre scene.

The Portland Hall

Although not in Portsmouth, brief mention should be made of this hall, for from 1860 until the King's Theatre was built in 1907, it was the only place of entertainment in Southsea.

It was situated in Kent Road, behind the Portland Hotel, and originally called "The Assembly Room." A Mr. William Davies, who also owned the Hotel, took over control of the hall in 1860, and renamed it the Portland Hall. In 1877, considerable improvements and renovations were carried out. It had a single balcony, and could seat around 800 patrons, it had 8 exits.

A variety of entertainments was presented:- recitals, concerts, lectures and plays. A poster, still hanging in the Portland Hotel, advertizes live plays presented in 1884; they were both adaptations from "The Pickwick Papers" by Charles Dickens.

Charles Hallé, Madame Norman Nerula and other well known artists appeared there. Even H.R.H. the Prince of Wales graced the Hall in 1882.

Poole's 'MYRIORAMA', a form of moving canvas pictures on rollers, was presented in the 1880s. This was a very popular form

Portland Hall, Kent Road, Southsea. This was located just behind the Portland Hotel. It was used for plays, concerts, balls and dinners, as shown in this photograph (probably early 1900s). K Edmonds-Gateley.

South Parade Pier Theatre – 1908. This attractive proscenium was destroyed when the stage was enlarged in 1933. K. Edmonds-Gateley.

of entertainment; it was also given in the Queen's Rooms, Lion Terrace.

In 1901, the Hall started to show films nightly; prices were from 3/- to 6d. This practice continued for a number of years. It finally closed in 1920.

New Grand Theatre, Southsea

This was yet another theatre that never was. A Southsea Theatre Syndicate was formed in 1900, and in January 1901, they applied for a licence.

The theatre was to be built on the corner of Elm Grove and the Thicket. They commissioned W. G. R. Sprague to design the building; he was one of the finest and most sensitive theatre architects at this period. Wyndham's Theatre, built 1899, shows Sprague at his best. The estimated cost was £40,000, a considerable sum in 1901.

The design was unusual, and a very elegant theatre would have resulted. The auditorium was to be circular – walls, circles, boxes would all be concentric. There was to have been orchestra stalls, pit, dress circle and a gallery; and crowned with an elaborate domed ceiling. Fine saloons were planned, including a magnificent crush bar measuring 30 feet by 25 feet.

The stage was to have a depth of 45 feet, and a width of 80 feet. The whole building would have been lit by electricty.

At the hearing, objections were heard from the residents of Elm Grove, which was then an extremely beautiful tree lined road, flanked by fine large houses. Many, such as North Grove House, were virtually small mansions in their own grounds. Understandably, Boughton, representing the Portsmouth Theatres Company, also lodged objections. The licence was refused on somewhat obscure legal grounds.

Later, in the same year, the Syndicate applied for a licence to build the theatre in Albert Road; this was also refused.

Doubtless Boughton, as owner of the Royal and Prince's, became perturbed over the possibility of new theatres springing up in the area. He strenuously fought against the proposed theatres in Elm Grove and Greatham Street, and also the planned New Empire Theatre in Stanhope Road. He countered these potential rivals by building a theatre of his own in Southsea – The King's Theatre.

South Parade Pier Theatre

The Pier Theatre, whilst again not in Portsmouth, did provide varied and good theatre for nearly 90 years.

The first Pier was opened in 1879, and destroyed by fire in 1904. There was a small theatre, or concert hall, on the far end.

On the 12th August, 1908, the new pier opened; it cost £70,000 and took six months to build. Apparently, the belief grew that the new pier was not safe; that it would collapse if too many people were on it at one time. In order to entice the wary public, and to prove their fears groundless, the Pier authorities advertized that, on a certain day, they would pay people to come on the pier. They did come,. hundreds of them! After this excellent piece of publicity, business flourished!

The aim from the start was for it to be 'select' and 'high class'; after all, it was near Craneswater! Consequently, the seats were relatively expensive, ranging from 2/- to 6d; a concert at the Clarence Pier only cost 2d in the cheapest seats.

The auditorium was most attractive. It was a rectangular hall, with a flat stalls floor, which could be used for dancing, and a single balcony wrapping round the three sides of the auditorium. The original proscenium arch was very fine, flanked on each side by reclining male figures. Their outstretched arms were linked by a festoon of gilded leaves, which draped above the arch. Their outer hands supported tridents. The elaborate pelmet and curtains were in deep crimson plush – a fragment of these curtains still exists, a cherished relic. It rose 'tableau' fashion.

The original stage was not very deep, and there were no flying facilities; all cloths had to be rolled. In the winter 1933–4, the stage was enlarged by extending it into the auditorium. This entailed the destruction of the beautiful proscenium; its replacement was very representative of the 1930s. It did not marry happily with the ornate plaster work of the remainder of the auditorium. A fly-tower and safety curtains were installed; six dressing rooms were constructed, plus one large chorus room.

In its early days, the pier aimed to rival the Theatre Royal, and London companies were frequently engaged. In 1912, for example, "Mr. John F. Preston, supported by Miss Mabelle F. Barlow and a Powerful London Company" presented "Nell Gwynne of Old Drury" and "The Three Musketeers". The scenery sounds impressive – six different sets for the first play, and ten for the second! No doubt, some of them were simply front cloths.

By the twenties, a pattern had been established. At Christmas, there was a professional pantomime. During the remainder of the winter, there were occasional professional and amateur companies. From Easter until mid-July, patrons were regaled with seasons of weekly-changing concert parties. From July until September, the Pier Theatre became a full scale touring date; many leading companies with straight plays and musical comedies were engaged. Included in these high-summer seasons were:- Maugham's "The Letter", "Brewster's Millions" and Hackett's comedy-thriller "77 Park Lane". On Sunday evenings, there were often symphony concerts.

The pier theatre originally seated about 1450; after the enlargement of the stage, this number was reduced to 1200.

Sadly, the auditorium and stage were completely destroyed by fire in 1976 whilst Ken Russell was filming "Tommy".

The New Prince's Theatre and The New Theatre Royal

Description of these theatres is left to last because, during the period being considered, they were the most famous, and the only 'straight' theatres in Town. From 1908, the South Parade Pier did present straight theatre, but at irregular intervals. Initially, under different ownerships, except for a short period in 1874, they competed for supremacy; from 1891 they came under the same direction – the Royal became "the major theatre in the south of England" and The Prince's became "The drama theatre of Portsmouth". Different artistic policies were adopted for each theatre.

Their very existence, and fame, depended on one man – John Waters Boughton.

A remarkable man, by any standard; he rebuilt the Royal twice (1884 and 1900), rebuilt the Prince's (1891) and caused the Kings to be built in 1907. From 1882, he alone directed the artistic and financial policy of these theatres, until his death in 1914.

His name first appears in the Town, as a flautist at the South of England Music Hall; he transferred to the Theatre Royal, and worked under Rutley.

A great man of the theatre, he was always searching for the best productions possible; in this quest he was supremely successful. He knew what his public liked and wanted, yet he was never afraid to engage the latest operas, tragedies and dramas.

With his wide theatrical contacts throughout England, he brought the finest actors of the period to his theatres. Every Twelfth Night, he went to the Theatre Royal, Drury Lane, for the Baddeley Cake Ceremony. (Robert Baddeley [1732 to 1794] left money to provide wine and cake in the Green Room of Drury

John Waters Boughton – the man who rebuilt the Theatre Royal twice, rebuilt the Prince's Theatre after a fire and built the King's Theatre. He formed the Portsmouth Theatres Company in 1897.

Lane every Twelfth Night. He was originally a cook; later he became an actor). This tradition still continues.

Each year at the Royal or Princes, he produced magnificent pantomimes; he searched all the year for novelties, new technical affects. The staging was lavish, with superb transformation scenes and costumes. They often lasted over four hours; patrons had their money's worth in those days.

It is clear from numerous articles in the *Portsmouth Times*, and from personal recollections, that he was greatly respected, and loyally served by his staff. It is to be remembered that in those halycon days, there would have been over a hundred people working in each theatre. He was a 'bon viveur', and an habitué of Monck's Oyster Bar in High Street; which was then almost a club for the prominent gentlemen of the Town.

He was also a kind, charitable man. Each year, for instance he would entertain the whole of the Portsmouth Gordon Boys Brigade at the Christmas Pantomime. Some 60 or 70 boys under the command of their Superintendent, Mr. Henry Harman, would march down to the Royal or Princes. Many of these boys were orphans, or came from poor homes. Boughton would also regale them with sweets and lemonade.

It was a very apt gesture, for these boys were often hired by pit patrons to take their place in the queue, until just before the doors opened. Depending on the show, the boys would queue up to three or four hours. The charge for a Gordon Boy in 1900 was 2d per hour!

In 1897, Boughton formed the Portsmouth Theatres Company, with himself as managing director. Presumably, more capital was required to renovate both theatres. Throughout the years, he was acquiring plots of land behind the Royal; likewise, he bought the Prince's site after the 1882 fire, and slowly acquired a vast area around that site. Hence he enlarged the Royal twice (1884 and 1900), and rebuilt the Prince's (1891) on a very much grander scale than the old one.

For some reason, he kept the initial negotiation concerning the building of the Kings Theatre secret from his Company. He intended it to be a straight theatre, but it was unsuccessful, and he soon turned it into a twice-nightly variety theatre. It was said that the relative failure of the King's Theatre contributed to his early death at 65.

His great legacy remains – the New Theatre Royal, playhouse and opera house; it is considered by experts to be one of the finest Victorian theatres surviving in the land.

The New Prince's Theatre, Lake Road, Landport

Its fortunes were variable in the first few years. It opened on 2nd January 1869 as a circus; circuses seemed to have been very popular. They were also presented at Ginnett's, Batty's and on a site in Lion Gate Road (now Edinburgh Road), which became the first Circus Church in 1857; and at one time in Landport Hall (later the Theatre Royal). The first season did not last long; it ended on 13th February. It re-opened in 1870 as the Royal Albert Theatre. Evidently it was not successful, for it again closed early in 1872. After some rebuilding and renovation, it re-opened on 11th November 1872 as the Prince's Theatre.

The building now consisted of:-

Private Boxes –	1½ and 1 guineas
Dress Circle with 200 comfortable chairs –	3/-
Pit with backed seats for 650 –	1/-
Gallery with 700 places	6d
(They must have been crammed!)	

Half price was after 9 o'clock.

There was a promenade for patrons in boxes and the dress circle.

The tier fronts were decorated with sprays of flowers, executed by T. Wilson, who also worked as a scenic artist at the South of England Music Hall. The ceiling had a large sunlight. Carpets and upholstery were from Maple's – very lush!

For the gala opening, a play "Masks and Faces" was presented, followed by a farce "How's Your Uncle".

A long opening oration was given by Miss Foote, one of the directors. A few verses will give an idea of these poetic offerings:-

Ladies and gentlemen, our bills express
This night, the promise of a short address.
And it's a genial and time-honoured mode,
With friends invited to a new abode,
To let a woman be the first to meet them,
And with a homely, hearty welcome, greet them.

We now revive the dear old custom; often
We hope the troubled path of life to soften.
'T will be our pleasure, and our constant care
To lay before you, good and wholesome fare.
But can we do it? Yes, we may foretell
That we will do it, honestly and well.

Behold our ship then launched upon the sea
Of public favour. How is it to be?
Is she to toss unheeded to the gale?
Or shall we prove there's no such word as fail?
Is she to drift upon the barren shore?
And be a thing of life and light no more!
Or shall she with crew, speed over the brine,

Royal Albert Theatre (later Prince's Theatre). Poster – early 1870s.

As rays of hope upon her pathway shine?
So like our gallant tars and soldiers true
We'll prove to you, if you'll to us be true blue.

Miss Foote then addressed each part of the house; the one for the pit is interesting:-

Now for the happy medium. Critics sit,
They always say, somewhere in the pit,
And seen are little faults. Oh, could I find you,
I'd take the chance this evening to remind you
That nothing human can be perfection,
A lady therefore seeks your kind protection.

Well the critics must have responded gallantly to the lady, for the ship did "speed over brine" until eventually shipwrecked on a fiery shore!

The productions were varied, and they must have been in constant competition with the Royal, the only other straight theatre in the town. It was also much larger, for it seated over 1500. The prices in the live theatres were much the same.

For Christmas 1873, the pantomime 'Columbus' was given. A dramatized version of "Domby and Son" was presented in March 1874; followed by a "Petite Comedy entitled 'Perfection'". Audiences (or managers) had interesting tastes in those days! In June 1874, Balfe brought his English Opera Company, and presented two of his own most popular operas. "The Rose of Castille" and "The Bohemian Girl". Balfe must have been a remarkable man; he wrote the operas, sang in them, produced them and had his own opera company. They were giants in those days! Later he often brought his company to the Royal. Another opera company also brought "Il Travatore" to the Prince's in 1874.

Sometimes the theatre seems to have been called the "Royal Prince's Theatre" during this period.

By the early 1880s, the artistic policy had changed; perhaps the Royal, re-vamped in 1874, had emerged the victor in the struggle for high class entertainment. It became known as "The Prince's Temperence Theatre of Varieties". There must have been a sigh of relief at the Royal! It does not seem to have been very successful, for there were many closures. Finally, on 24th April 1882, the 'ship' finally came to grief; it was destroyed by fire.

A Mrs. Gillam, who lived opposite, informed the Portsmouth Times that she went to her window at 4.50 am, and saw flames bursting out through the top left hand window. Then the roof caught fire at 6.00 am. It (the heat) was so intense, that she could no longer stand at the window.

She also reported that earlier, 20 minutes to 1 am to be precise, she heard a shot from inside the theatre. (She must have had a restless night!). Oddly nothing more was heard of this strange 'shot'; the imagination bubbles with superb possibilities!

The Chief Fireman told the reporter:- "It is right to add that the thickness of the walls doubtless contributed to the escape of other properties. For had it been of similar construction to the Hippodrome in Bow Street, the Brigade would have been heavily handicapped in their exertions." Ginnett's New Hippodrome, adjacent to the Town Station, was a wooden structure at this time.

The New Prince's Theatre

Boughton acquired site of the old theatre, and slowly bought up adjacent plots. By 1891, he had a site with a frontage of 95 feet, flanked on one side by a Baptist Chapel. There was an outlet into Alexandra Road, behind the tavern. It had a total depth of 194 feet, the extremity being in North Town Street, a cul-de-sac. The theatre was designed by Frank Matcham, and built by F. D. Hall of Portsmouth in 128 days, an extraordinary feat.

The Baptist Chapel opposed the granting of a licence, and at the hearing, their solicitor commented "on the danger which would

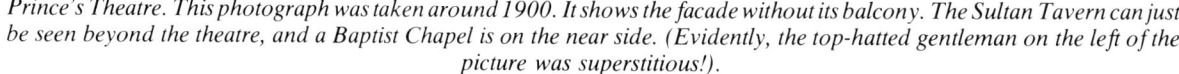

Prince's Theatre. This photograph was taken around 1900. It shows the facade without its balcony. The Sultan Tavern can just be seen beyond the theatre, and a Baptist Chapel is on the near side. (Evidently, the top-hatted gentleman on the left of the picture was superstitious!).

THE NEW PRINCE'S THEATRE, LANDPORT.

Prince's Theatre, Lake Road, Portsmouth. A sketch of the elevation; architect – Frank Matcham, 1891.
A cast-iron balcony was erected in front of the building in 1907; it was similar to the balcony at the Royal
which was erected in 1900.

Prince's Theatre – proscenium arch, boxes and tiers.

Prince's Theatre, Lake Road. The cast of the Stock Company on the occasion of the 600th performance.

Prince's Theatre – a packed house for the 600th performance by the Repertory Company.

occur from the moral point of view, which cannot be disputed. Also there is the danger of actors outside the theatre." Evidently, the worthy Baptists thought theatre was an agency for Satan. In spite of these objections, the licence was granted; doubtless, Boughton's great record at the Royal influenced the magistrates.

The theatre opened on Boxing Day 1891, with the pantomime "Dick Whittington".

The Portsmouth Times gave a detailed account of its appearance. The prevailing colours were blue, cream, with terra-cotta shading, and a profusion of gilt. The curtaining and hangings were old gold, the dress circle seating old gold and blue. Busts of Shakespeare and Beethoven flanked the proscenium arch, whilst the Prince of Wales Feathers and diadem formed the crown. Gilded panels radiated from a central sunlight in the ceiling; each panel contained the name of a noted author or composer. Auditorium and stage were lit by gas; open scroll work around the ceiling gasoliers helped to give ventilation – this was most essential in gas-lit theatres. The stage lighting was controlled on the "Flash Light Principle", by which every gas light could be brought into use with "the twinkling of an eye". The spacious stage had a lofty fly tower.

Originally it sat about 2,000. By 1912 the capacity was

	4 boxes	16	originally the whole of the ground floor was pit.
Stalls		353	
	Pit	248	
1st Tier	Circle	108	These two areas were separated by a partition, both on the same tier.
	Upper Circle	230	
2nd Tier	Gallery		Again, this tier was divided by a partition. Later the upper part was converted to a saloon.
	Upper Gallery	500	

Both tiers were of wooden construction, but all staircases were made of concrete and were fireproof; all emergency exits led direct into the open.

The 'galleryites' had their own entrance through a covered sideway, between the theatre and the chapel. All other patrons used one main entrance foyer, and box office.

Artistic Policy

Boughton's policy for the Prince's Theatre was to engage touring companies presenting drama, and above all, melodrama. Contemporary opinion derides melodrama, but it was highly popular throughout Europe during this period, and the best examples can still hold an audience today. The Christmas Pantomime would sometimes be given at the Prince's, whilst the Royal would then have a musical or light opera. During the reconstruction of the Royal in 1900, all its normal shows went to the Prince's.

Renovations to the Prince's Theatre – 1907

Matcham was re-engaged to supervise the renovations. By cantilevering, an extra row of seats was added to the existing dress circle. De Jong, of London, designed and executed the new plaster work for the boxes and panels in the tiers.

Fine mahogany doors, fitted with bevelled glass, were fitted, stairways carpeted; new curtaining and upholstery were in scarlet. Seven rows of orchestra stalls were introduced at the front of the old pit area. The auditorium was redecorated in cream and gold, relieved by pale green. The whole theatre was then re-lit with electricity.

The cast-iron balcony, very similar to that at the Royal, was erected along the entire 93 foot frontage; all the windows were fitted with attractively designed stained glass. These large cast iron balconies were fairly uncommon; the balcony at the Royal is probably the sole survivor in this country.

Prince's Theatre. The wrecked theatre in 1940 after a direct hit during an afternoon air raid. The photograph gives an idea of the facade with the cast-iron balcony of 1907. The similarity with the Theatre Royal can be seen; the Royal balcony was added in 1900.

The Prince's new balcony provided ample space for new lounges. A lounge for ladies and a tea room, both "charmingly decorated" were constructed on the first tier level, and a new saloon on the second tier level.

Boughton now possessed three fine large theatres: the Theatre Royal, enlarged in 1900; the Prince's Theatre and the King's Theatre which opened in 1907. Peter Davey took control of the company on Boughton's death in 1914; initially, he kept very much to the same artistic policy. From 29th November 1920, a resident repertory company occupied the Prince's. They must have been successful, for they lasted for 107 weeks, 646 nights and gave 1292 performances, reckoned to have been a record at that time. Amongst the cast were: Beryl Adair, leading lady; J. Grant Anderson, juvenile lead (and matinée idol); Milton C. Curtain, the villain; Charles Denville and John Laurie.

Every hundredth night was treated as a gala night, and at the end of the performance, the entire stage staff and management also came on stage. Page 42 shows the audience for the 600th night; a sight to bring joy to the most pessimistic manager! An orchestra of three, who were reputed to be able to play any instrument, delighted audiences with extracts from operas and musicals.

The Company lasted at the Prince's until 13 January 1923, when they moved to a theatre – previously a cinema – in High Street, Gosport. (The building is now a radio shop – Rumbelows Ltd.)

The finale was approaching; there was a four week variety season, followed by a short season of touring companies. It finally closed as a theatre on 2nd June 1924.

Peter Davey had retired by then, and Mr. W. E. C. Sperring became Managing Director of the Portsmouth Theatres.

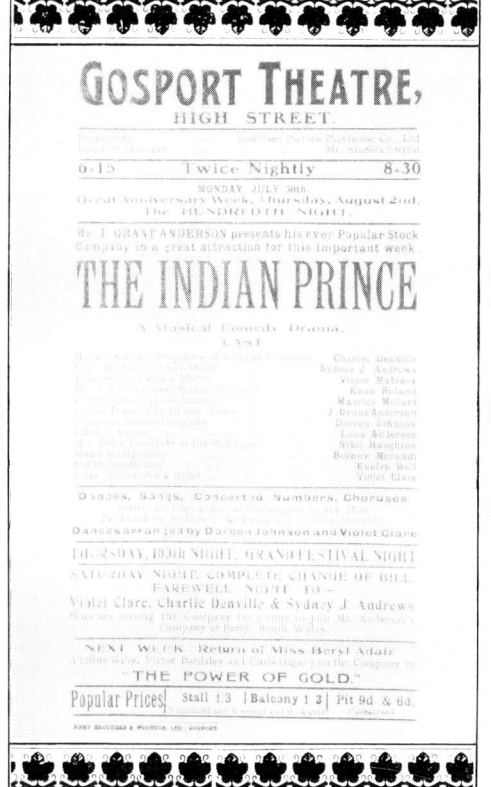

Gosport Theatre, High Street, Gosport. The season was presented by the Stock Company from the Prince's Theatre in Lake Road. Unfortunately the venture did not last very long. Rumbelows now occupy the building.

Mr. J. Grant Anderson – leading actor with the resident repertory company at the Prince's Theatre 1922/3. He later led the company at the Gosport Theatre and South Parade Pier Theatre.

The theatre was rented to Mr. S. Zeid, who re-opened it as a cinema. Initially, there was rear projection, but in 1930 the gallery was closed and a projection box installed at the rear of the gallery. The theatre was sold to Joe Davison of Charlotte Street, a cinema proprietor, for £30,000 in 1930.

In 1931, the interior was gutted; boxes, tiers were all removed, and one large balcony constructed. Internally, it thus resembled any other purpose built cinema.

Ghosts could still wander disconsolately across the vast stage behind the silver screen, and linger in vacated dressing rooms. Ghosts of 'toppers' could still lounge in the dusty saloons. A few relics – posters, programmes, photographs and press-pass disc – are the only tangible relics of the fine theatre.

The end came during a matinée on 24th August 1940, when it was severely damaged by a bomb.

The Theatre Royal
The Beginning
There was nothing between the Landport Gate and the Swan Tavern in the early 1800s, except for the Mill Pond, and the meadows surrounding the Tavern. Eventually a few houses were erected on the Gate side of the Tavern, and the fine square, Nelson Square, came into being. Next to the Tavern, a racquets court was built, owned by the Tavern. Later, the court was converted into a hall, called the Landport Hall. By the late 1840s, the Ordnance had built a large house just behind the Tavern. There was also a builder's yard and some stables. Much of this area was eventually incorporated into the site of the present theatre.

The First Theatre
In 1854, Mr. Henry Rutley, a travelling circus proprietor came

Theatre Royal. The facade of the first theatre on the present site, after the erection of "The new and elegantly designed conservatory on Winter Gardens" over a colonnade in front of the theatre in 1874. The old Swan Tavern is on the left, and a sawmill was on the right.

47

to Portsmouth, and took over the Swan Tavern (later the White Swan) and the adjacent Landport Hall. He installed his circus in the Hall, and it proved a financial success.

In February 1856, he applied for a licence to convert the Hall into a theatre; this application was granted, initially for a period of nine months, subject to all communicating doors with the Tavern being bricked up. Rutley hoped his proposed theatre would become "a public place of amusement to which the middle classes of the Borough might resort."

By this time, the old Theatre Royal in High Street had been demolished to make way for the new Cambridge Barracks, and the Landport Theatre (formerly the Grecian Saloon) went bankrupt in 1850. Thus, there was no straight theatre in the area at this time.

On the 29th September, 1856, the theatre opened with 'A New Way to Pay Old Debts', a popular comedy act written in 1621 by Philip Massinger. The leading actor in this production, William Shalders, had been 'acting manager' in the old High Street theatre; thus a link with the past was kept. A number of other actors also came with him, and, like him, had appeared at the Landport Theatre.

According to the 'Portsmouth Times' of 4th October, 1856:- "The Hall has undergone a complete transformation in the construction of a theatre, which is comfortable and commodious in every part. The decorations of the various parts of the theatre, and the painting of the scenes, are very good, and are, indeed, far above the average. On the opening night every part of the theatre was crowded to excess, and numbers were refused admittance. Every arrangement is made by Mr. Rutley to preserve order, and to secure the comfort of those who frequent this place of entertainment".

The frontage was about 40 feet, with a simple arcade over the pavement. On the north side of the building was a steam sawmill,

Theatre Royal. The painting, at the top of the grand staircase, before and after restoration. A plaque states it came from "the old Theatre Royal" – presumably the 1856 building. Artist is unknown. Originally it formed part of the proscenium crown.

whilst on the opposite corner was a coach manufactory.

The auditorium had two circles and numerous boxes. As early as 1871, limes were in use. A detail from the painting forming the proscenium crown is hung at the head of the present main staircase. It depicts two reclining muses supporting the masks of tragedy and comedy (page 48). The canvas later suffered severe damage in the 1950s by the Management's stapling forthcoming events on it. It has recently been restored by Mr. Ambrose Scott Moncrieff, at the expense of a devoted lover of the Theatre Royal.

Rutley presented a wide range of entertainment. Opera must have been popular, for many posters of the period record opera companies appearing at the Theatre. The most frequently presented included:- ''Don Giovanni'', ''Faust'', ''Martha'', ''Fra Diovolo'', ''La Sonnambula'' and ''The Bohemian Girl''. Balfe, who wrote the latter opera, was a frequent visitor; he brought his own opera company to perform his operas. A repertoire of Shakespeare's plays were frequently given. All these works were usually followed by a laughable farce. I suppose you could leave the theatre, if such an offering did not please you after ''Macbeth'' or ''Faust''! At times there was a resident repertory company.

In 1872, a number of improvements were carried out; possibly to counter the alterations of the re-vamped Prince's Theatre. The cast iron balcony was erected over the pavement arcade (page 47); backing was provided to pit benches. A large mirror was placed at the top of the main staircase; it is thought that the mirror which adorns the present dress circle arcade could well be the same one.

Prices for opera and other major companies in the 1860s were:-

Private Boxes	$1\frac{1}{2}$ and 1 guinea
Stalls (these were circle stalls)	5/-
Front Boxes	4/-
Side Boxes	2/-
Pit	1/-
Gallery	6d

Smoking was strictly prohibited for opera.

Amateur performances, produced mainly by the services, were frequent; their programmes were printed on silk, and superbly designed.

It is to be remembered that Portsmouth and the new resort of Southsea, contained many wealthy residents, including nobility and royalty. Prince Maurice von Saxe-Weimar lived in what is now the Mayville Hotel. Portsmouth was rated the fifth richest town in England. There was money about. Hence Rutley, and later Boughton, could engage the best actors and companies available, and charge the relatively high seat prices. It was also part of the social round to hear the Opera, and see the Play.

Rutley died in 1874; his wife carried on for a short time, and then the theatre closed until 1875. The ''Portsmouth and Southsea Assembly Rooms and Theatres Limited'' obtained possession, and operated the Royal for a few years.

By 1882 Boughton had taken over the Theatre, and considered that the converted racquets court no longer sufficed. He started to buy up small parcels of land around the old theatre. He decided on a complete rebuild, and engaged Phipps to design his grand new theatre. Charles John Phipps was one for the finest, and most sensitive of the Victorian theatre architects, and influenced considerably by European design. William Ward of Fratton was appointed builder.

The last production in the first theatre was ''Les Manteaux Noirs'', a comic opera by Yorke in May 1884. On the 19th May, the demolition commenced. The outer walls of the much larger new structure had been built around the old theatre, so as to reduce the closure time to a minimum. Nothing visible remains of the first theatre, except part of the dressing room block and, perhaps, one window of the old façade now forming one wall of a toilet in the present first tier.

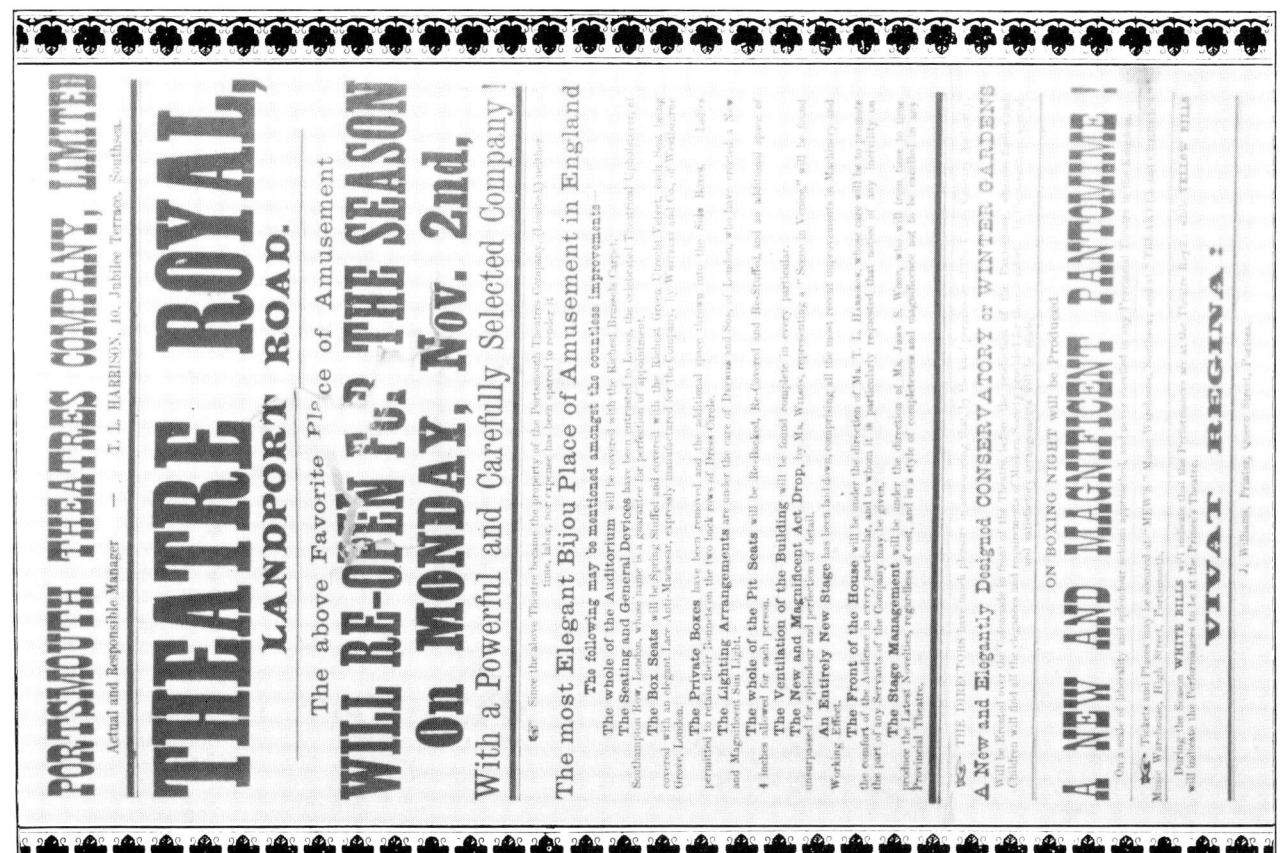

Theatre Royal – part of a playbill of November 1874, listing the improvements made. It is interesting to note the existence of a "Portsmouth Theatres Company Ltd.", which apparently also controlled the Prince's Theatre. This arrangement lasted only a short time, and occurred soon after Rutley's death, when the theatre went through a difficult period; it was closed at various times.

The Second Theatre (called the New Theatre Royal)

The Theatre re-opened on 4th August, 1884, with "Princess Ida". The principals were professionals from the D'Oyly Carte Opera Company, officers of the Garrison sang other roles, supported by an amateur chorus of 100 and the Royal Marine Artillery Band.

The Evening News reported that:- "A more brilliant scene than the opening of the New Theatre Royal has not occurred in the annals of Portsmouth for some time. There was about it all the pomp, pride and pageantry which seems appropriate to such an occasion. It had almost the dignity of a high state function."

The military C-in-C, General Willis, and his wife were present in a private box, and the theatre was packed.

Boughton, who became Manager in 1882, and later formed the Portsmouth Theatres Ltd in 1897, gave the opening oration:-

"The ancient Portsmouth Playhouse disappears,
That served its purpose here for many years,
But there is reason in the adage true,
The order Old e'er yield to the New,
And thus the building takes it place,
And looks the public fairly in the face.
Not spared have been my money, work and pains,
To crown the edifice with you remains,
By patronage like that of yore – no less,
But even more – I'm sure then of success.
Fam'd Irving soon, I hope will visit here,
And with fair Ellen Terry will appear;
Sarah Bernhardt, of Paris long the rage,
I also trust ere long will grace our stage.'

Boughton was lucky – the crowds did flock to his lovely new building, and all the hoped-for great actors did grace his stage.

The second theatre had three tiers, and three boxes, one above

Theatre Royal. The interior of the 1884 theatre, designed by Phipps. This artists impression was reproduced in a programme. The proscenium arch is located where the present boxes are. In 1900, the old boxes were removed, the two upper tiers extended, and the first tier rebuilt. K. Edmonds-Gateley.

the other, flanked each side of the proscenium arch. There were two boxes at the rear of the first tier. The proscenium arch was located where the boxes in the present theatre start. The decor was white and gold, and the various murals were painted by Ballard.

The ground floor was entirely occupied by the pit, with cushioned benches; the dress circle had armchairs, "to allow for the increasing amplitude of ladies dresses". The seating in the Gods is not described! The Theatre had a capacity of 2000. The Stage was 40 feet deep, with a proscenium opening of 30 feet.

Although the façade of Phipps' building is still retained, the entrances were entirely different. Next to the Tavern there was a 'private entrance' leading to the boxes and first tier; then came two entrances for the general public to the same areas. There was a simple portico for these entrances, to allow patrons to enter the theatre in the dry from their carriages. There was a small saloon above the portico – for gentlemen! The fourth entrance was to the upper circle, whilst the fifth led into the pit. The gallery entrance was at the rear in Spring Gardens Lane, which in those days continued round the back of the Theatre to the Swan Tavern.

The whole theatre was lit by gas. The telephone was installed in 1885.

The term 'New' Theatre Royal is not unique, many others had the prefix 'New' after rebuilding. Likewise, the title 'Opera House'; they did indeed frequently present opera, but were not designed specifically for opera. In particular, the orchestra pits were usually completely inadequate for opera orchestras.

Within 16 years, Boughton decided to enlarge the auditorium, and improve the stage facilities. This time he engaged Frank Matcham to re-design the Royal, the two men had already worked together on the Prince's Theatre in 1891.

The Third Theatre (the present building)

In April 1900 the theatre closed, and all shows booked went to the Prince's Theatre. The reconstruction was carried out by J. Cooke of Southsea; a firm which continued to operate until the 1940s. De Jong of London was responsible for the plaster work, and Whiteheads did the marble, both of whom employed mainly Italians for these tasks.

Phipp's building was retained, except for the boxes and proscenium arch; these made way for the present double tiered boxes and new proscenium arch. The new stage was extended across Spring Gardens Lane and into the properties beyond, which Boughton had acquired over the years. Its full depth is 65 feet, an enormous size, and one of the largest in the provinces. The dress circle was entirely reconstructed with fire proof materials and the plaster work was renewed throughout the building.

The old portico was removed, and the present cast iron balcony erected. New entrances were made, all faced with magnificent polished granite, and surmounted by very fine sgraphitto panels. A figure of Neptune, complete with a gas flambeau, graced the pediment.

On the 6th August 1900 the reconstructed theatre re-opened with the drama 'MAGDA' by Sudermann. Mrs. Patrick Campbell gave the oration and also played the title role in the play. With her in the play were George Arliss and Gerald du Maurier. As often in those days, a one-act play preceded the main play. The curtain raiser on this occasion was 'Mrs. Jordan – Actress'. Curiously and appropriately, the opening lines of the play, spoken by the maid as she entered the room were "La, what a lovely place". The fine baroque-rococo auditorium filled to capacity, nearly 2000 persons, must have presented a magnificent and beautiful sight. The Governor Mayor, officers in full dress and bejewelled ladies filled the boxes, dress circle and orchestra stalls.

The colour scheme of the auditorium was cream, heavily

Theatre Royal. An early photograph, soon after its enlargement in 1900, showing the theatre in its full beauty. The division between orchestra stalls and pit can be seen. The fine conductors stand and orchestra pit rail have alas disappeared.

ornamented with gold leaf, and terra cotta. Rich, gold-embroidered, scarlet curtains adorned the boxes and dress circle arcades. The great scarlet stage curtain, heavily decorated with embroidery and gold thread, rose in tableau fashion to reveal an Act Drop showing HMS Victory being drawn into Harbour by Fame and attendant cherubs. Above the proscenium arch is the sole remaining mural – depicting Melpomene surrounded by boys, some of whom, carrying a large terrifying mask, are frightening the others. The mural is a large convex-concave panel, supported by an arcade of engaged corinthian columns, and flanked by a pair of superb winged cherubs, blowing long trumpets.

The ceiling plaster work, designed as a wheel, has delicate rococo ornamentation which contained canvases showing putti disporting in the skies, defying gravity. They, together with some fine crystal light bowls, were eliminated during various redecorations. The ceiling is raked, a unique feature, in order to improve the sight lines for those in the back of the third tier, and this also aids the superb acoustic qualities of the auditorium.

The boxes, framed by marble pillars, bear military and naval symbols, and are surmounted by framed wheel traceries, before which stand heroic Greek busts on plinths.

The first tier panels are decorated with naval symbols – mermaids, dolphins, anchors, the sea and shells. The brass light fittings were in the form of anchors, which supported light globes. The second tier panels honour the military, with laurel-wreathed lion heads, and putti holding crowns with draped guidons and colours. The scrolls between the putti were gold leafed, and painted on them were swags of foliage, musical instruments and fruits. These too have been destroyed. The third tier panels have deeply moulded plaster work, decorated with typical S and C rococo motifs.

The Dress Circle saloon and smoking room in the balcony over the pavement were reserved for gentlemen. The ladies had, however, a separate boudoir at one end of the balcony. It is interesting to note the productions at the other Portsmouth Theatres during the opening week:-

Princes Theatre (Rebuilt 1891) 'Alone in London' with Ada Elliston
Empire Theatre (Built in 1892) 'The Relief at Mafeking'
People's Palace (Built in 1884) 'The Battle of Life'

The following productions were presented during 1900 at the Royal:-

'Message from Mars'
'The Degenerates' with Mrs. Langtry
'The Geisha'
'D'Oyly Carte Opera'
'Cinderella', which lasted over four hours!

In rapid succession the great actors adorned its vast stage – Ellen Terry, Sarah Bernhardt, Henry Irving, Wilson Barrett, Martin Harvey, Matheson Lang, Frank Benson and his Shakespearian Company, Gladys Cooper, Fred Terry, Julia Nelson, Sybil Thorndike, John Gielgud, and so many others. To write about them all, would be to write a history of the English stage from the 1850s to the 1920s.

Opera seasons lasting a month were frequent; the companies included Rouseby's English Opera Company and the Royal Carl Rosa Company. 'Aida' and 'The Flying Dutchman' were amongst the spectacular operas presented. The annual pantomime was always a magnificent event, which included gorgeous transformation scenes, whilst demons made full use of the cunning stage lifts. It was usually at the Royal, but some years Boughton would present a musical at the Royal for Christmas, and put the pantomime into the Prince's Theatre. The 'stage roller' enable horses to gallop across the stage.

Theatre Royal – staircase to Boxes, Dress Circle and Orchestra Stalls. The semi-circular painting from the 1856 theatre can be seen at head of stairs. (Photo dates from 1960s).

Early posters requested gentlemen to instruct their coachmen to set them down with the horses' heads facing the Station, and to take them up with the horses' heads facing the recreation ground – the wealthy lived in Southsea! For the less wealthy, cycles were stored free during performances.

In 1902 the prices of seats were

Boxes	1½ and 1 guinea
Dress Circle and Stalls	4/-
Upper Circle	2/-
Pit	1/-
Gallery	6d

The prices had not changed since the 1860s; no inflation in those stable days!

Soldiers in uniform, together with their families, were allowed in at half price – no mention is made of sailors! The ordinary public were allowed in at half price at 9.30 pm.

Mr. Dick Merewood, who was Call Boy in 1903, recently recorded his memoirs of those days. His salary was 2/6d per week, supplemented by tips from the chorus girls, who used to send him out to fetch a quart of gin at 3/6. They told him, they needed it for their voices! Irving, by this time, had very poor eyesight, and he would place his hand on the Call Boy's head, who would lead him to the stage.

He contrasted the splendour of the auditorium with the dark gas-lit corridors and staircases of the Dressing Room Block. This block is the oldest extant part of the theatre, and the central portion almost certainly served the original 1856 theatre. When the theatre went over to variety, the dressing rooms were named, instead of being numbered. No. 1 Victory, No. 2 Nelson, whilst the others were named after theatrical people, Rutley, Irving, Marie Lloyd, Dan Leno etc.

Irving's last visit to the Theatre Royal was in January 1905,

Theatre Royal – a fine iron moulding of Poseidon – a detail from a panel in the cast-iron balcony.

56

when he stayed at the Royal Pier Hotel, then the best in town. Queues for the early pit used to stretch from the Theatre right down, and round the gas office corner. In those days, they used to pack 2000 people into the Royal.

Sarah Bernhardt on one of her frequent visits to the Theatre, scribbled on the wall of Boughton's office, "MERCI, AU PLUS CHARMANT DIRECTEUR SARAH BERNHARDT
9 JUILLET 1902"

'Flying Matinées' were frequent. The principals would travel down from London in the morning, do the matinée, and return to Town for the evening performance. (The steam train did the journey in 1 hour 50 minutes before the 1914 War). The harrassed stage manager had to produce from his own stock the required settings and properties.

The equally harrassed electrician would have to rig a simple lighting plot. Often the minor roles were taken by local people. Such improvisations would probably be unacceptable to present audiences. However, these flying matinées were hugely successful, and enabled provincials to see the great actors. There was a flying matinée of 'Madame Butterfly' at the Hippodrome in 1908, complete with a cast of 80 and an orchestra of 35!

By the late 20s, the position for all theatres was desperate; vastly increased costs after the 1914–1918 war, and the advent of talkies and to some extent of the radio, caused theatres to close throughout the country. There were ever fewer companies on the road. The Prince's Theatre was already rented out as a cinema; the King's Theatre had shown films in the afternoons since the mid-twenties, and eventually went over to films entirely.

The Denville Players, a repertory company, moved into the Theatre Royal in 1930.

Seats were even cheaper than in the 1860s, but it should be observed that the Denville Company played 'twice nightly'.

Theatre Royal – the fine wheel ceiling; the panels originally possessed painting of clouds and flying cherubs. Cut glass globes twinkled between each panel. (Photograph taken 1970).

Boxes	$\frac{1}{2}$ guinea
Stalls	1/8 and 1/3
Dress circle	1/3
Upper circle	10d
Early pit	7d
Pit	6d
Balcony	4d

Their last performance was on 5th March 1932. As the audience was filing out on that final night, a schoolboy, so distressed at its closure as a theatre, protested loudly as he drew level with Irving's portrait in the arcade of the dress circle. The audience around him joined the protest, and although nothing changed as a result of this spontaneous outcry, a protest – the first –had been made.

On the 7th March, the theatre opened for an ''All Star Talkie Season''. A pantomime, 'Dick Whittington', was given for Christmas 1933, after which films were again shown. The projection box was at the rear of the stage, so giving 'rear' projection. Films continued until 1948.

After a disastrous redecoration, when all the paintings, Victorian lighting and fittings were swept away, the theatre re-opened as a variety theatre. Initially it did very well; but eventually tottered to closure in October 1956. Mr. K. Edmonds Gateley, who 24 years previously had been the protesting schoolboy, and now Director of the Southsea Shakespeare Actors, wrote a letter to the News. Published under the title ''Royal must not be demolished'', the letter appealed to the City Council to buy it, and make it a civic theatre. It aroused considerable attention, and approval.

However, in 1957 the theatre re-opened as a repertory theatre, under the direction of Kim Peacock and Hector Ross. They played a weekly repertory system, and presented a varied selec-

tion of some very fine plays. In 1959, the company moved to the King's Theatre. From 1960 to 1966, wrestling was presented; the ring, and ring seats, being on stage. The King's pantomime was transferred to the Royal in January 1966; this was the last live performance in the theatre.

It was generally understood, that the owners wished to demolish the building and re-develop the site. A Councillor, backed by two colleagues, approached Mr. K. Edmonds Gateley, and asked him to initiate a new, vigorous campaign to save the theatre. Thus, the final long campaign was started, and he managed to whip up considerable support both in the city, and nationally.

Meanwhile the building was deserted; thieves broke in and stole every piece of brass and lead that could possibly be removed. Squatters and others lived in the place for some time, leaving it in a stygian state.

The Theatre Royal Society was founded in 1970, as a result of a letter to the News from some members of St. John's College. It was through a small devoted band of volunteers, that the theatre survived the next decade.

Then came two savage blows. In November 1972, children broke in and fired rockets on the stage, so causing a fire which destroyed the stage roof and technical block. The Fire Brigade performed miracles, and so saved the auditorium; the dropping of the safety curtain also helped. Finally in the Spring of 1973, a few 'yobs' broke in, and in the course of an afternoon smashed statues, plaster works and windows. To the first observer who saw the damage, it looked as if a bomb had been exploded; it was a terrible, tragic sight.

In 1980, upon the liquidation of the Portsmouth Theatres Company, the New Theatre Royal Trust Company purchased the Theatre. This Trust Company is an off-shoot from the Theatre Royal Society.

It is to be hoped that this 'Sleeping Beauty', as Iain Mackintosh

Theatre Royal restoration. Artist Eve Tipler painstakingly removing layers of paint from the fine plaster moulding in foyer.

The fire which destroyed the stage and technical wing in November 1972. It was caused by children, who had broken into the building, playing with fireworks.

Theatre Royal Restoration. Wyn Bradey spent a year, with other helpers, removing six layers of paint which had been applied to the magnificent mahogany doors in the foyer.

61

Theatre Royal – panels of first tier, showing naval motifs.

called her, will be restored to her former glory, with a rebuilt stage incorporating all the latest technical aids.

Then Boughton's finest theatre can function, once more, as a lyric and dramatic theatre.

Development of Theatre Architecture and the Theatre Royal

It is interesting to note that the Theatre Royal, partly due to the 1900 modifications, illustrates the evolution of theatre architecture, from its inception in the 17th century in Italy, until the end of the 19th century.

In the early theatres, tiered shallow boxes filled the circular or horse-shoe shaped auditorium. The eight boxes in the Theatre Royal are typical examples of such boxes.

Early in the 19th century, they began to construct deeper tiers, with rows of seats, which began to 'fly' out towards the stage. They were supported on iron pillars, which continued through each tier down to the ground floor. The second and third tiers of the Theatre Royal, constructed in 1884, are examples of this type. They are built entirely of wood, highly complex in structure and depend on pillars going down to the stalls floor.

By the end of the 19th century, the balconies were constructed with steel and concrete, and, by a system of cantilevering, balconies could fly far out into the auditorium without the aid of pillars. The first tier of the Royal, constructed in 1900, is an example.

The very fine plaster work in the Theatre Royal is typical of the baroque-rococo style, which continued in the theatre long after it had been deserted for other types of building. In the 17th and 18th centuries, ornamentations were carried in carved stone, marble or wood; and fine examples still survive in Bavaria, Austria and Italy. Later, the decorative work was moulded in plaster, often prefabricated and made in separate panels.

Thus, the Theatre Royal illustrates the development of theatre architecture and gives superb and exuberant examples of baroque decor.

Technical Data
Stage Depth   65 feet
Proscenium Opening 31 feet
8 Dressing rooms, plus 2 chorus dressing rooms
Width of auditorium 62 feet

There were 49 sets of lines on the grid.

The King's Theatre

Like the Portland Hall, it is not in Portsmouth, but mention should be made of it.

The initial planning was carried out secretly by Boughton, possibly because of the delicate problem of purchasing the required property. Interestingly, the 'Twinnies' were in the secret; they were the two sisters who ran Monck's restaurant.

The theatre was designed by Matcham and built by Corke – the same team responsible for the 1900 re-building of the Royal. Matcham was faced with a difficult task, because of the peculiar shape of the land available. He was adept, however, at solving such problems, for he had been often faced with similar situations. It did eliminate the possibility of a fine façade. It took 12 months to build; the time required for such work was becoming longer!

The main foyer stands on the site of Ebenezer Perkin's grocery shop in Albert Road, Southsea and the stage area was built over a spring. On occasions, below stage still has to be pumped clear of water.

The theatre was opened on 30th September 1907 by Henry Irving's son, Mr. H. B. Irving, who brought some of the plays in which his father had achieved so much fame. They included, 'Charles 1st' and 'The Lyon's Mail'. Irving père had died late in 1905. The Theatre Royal orchestra was in the pit.

Matcham's design for the Kings was not one of his best, and signs of decadence in style are apparent. The auditorium, however, is still impressive.

The main colours were cream and gold, with seating in green plush.

According to the Portsmouth Times, busts of famous people adorned the dome; included were Shakespeare, Dickens, George Eliot, Mozart and Beethoven. These have disappeared, probably during the redecorations in the 1920s; paintings now adorn the dome. The ceiling fresco in the foyer, also executed at that time, portray the features of two local beauties of the day.

The alabaster proscenium arch is crowned by a cumbrous cartouche, supported by putti; in all, a somewhat unbalanced feature. The boxes all partly face the audience; a feature that was becoming too frequent.

Sadly, it was not a success as a drama theatre, and Boughton reluctantly introduced twice nightly variety from the 3rd August 1908

Costs of seats at that time were:-

Lower Boxes	$\frac{1}{2}$ guinea
Upper Boxes	2/- per seat
Stalls	1/- and 6d
Grand Circle	6d
Pit	6d and 4d
Gallery	3d and 2d

The Reverend Bruce Cornford, who built the magnificent St. Matthew's Church in Fawcett Road, used to hold great Services of Witness on Good Fridays in the theatre.

The King's fell to films even before the Prince's. In the early

King's Theatre, Southsea. A photograph soon after erection, and before it became a variety theatre. It was built on the site of Perkin's grocery store; the stage is located over a spring.

King's Theatre, Southsea. An early photograph looking very attractive with its ornate borders and curtains.

65

20s, films were shown in the afternoons, and music hall in the evenings. Later, there were often film weeks; films being shown at both matinées and evenings.

In 1931, and operating box was created in the balcony, and 'Talkies' were presented from October 1931.

In 1932, it reverted to a theatre, when the Royal went over to films.

Seating in 1907:-

Stalls	460
Pit	336
Circle	204
Upper Circle	418
Gallery	724
Boxes	30
TOTAL	2172

Henry Rutley. He acquired the Swan Tavern and Landport Hall in 1854. In 1856 he converted the hall into the first Theatre Royal on that site.

Theatre Royal – Mrs. Patrick Campbell, who gave the oration in 1900, when the theatre re-opened after enlargement. She also played the lead in "Magda" by Sudermann.

Theatre Royal programme cover, 1908.

Theatre Royal. Sir Henry Irving; he appeared many times in the theatre. This portrait hangs in the arcade of the first tier. It was missing for many years, and was finally found by the author in the cellar of a house in Auckland Road West! Southsea.

EPILOGUE

The collection of material for this work has been an excursion into the past – fascinating even exciting. Slowly, it was revealed how rich the theatrical scene was in the last century. The accounts in the Portsmouth Times, posters, programmes, photographs, tickets all brought the past to the present. One really felt as if one knew these theatres – most now completely forgotten; a picture was conjured in the imagination, and one could envisage sitting in various theatres, or prowling backstage. The Prince's Theatre, of the lost ones, perhaps came most vividly to life, because of the recollections of many who are still alive. Laurie Upton, above all, brought back the Prince's Theatre, with his vivid memory, and the precious relics he possesses of that theatre.

No doubt, much of the entertainment would be decried by contemporary standards, and most likely much of it was, in fact, technically poor. But it entertained people; it was another world – whether opera, tragedy, comedy or Music Hall.

Only a glimpse of the life which throbbed in these theatres can be given here; a life created by all those who worked there – actors, chorus girls, jugglers, stage-managers, call boys, the lot.

Above all, 'life' throbbed because of 'Theatre' – the great tragedies and comedies which were enacted in them. It is indeed not "the business of the dramatist to bring life to the theatre, but to bring the theatre to life." (Cocteau)

It is to be hoped that the Theatre Royal – the finest jewel of them all, and Boughton's masterpiece – will be restored to its former beauty and its pre-eminence as a theatre. It will then be the splendid heir to, and the vicarious representative of, its long lost peers.

The author would be most grateful if any errors were reported to him via the publishers. He would also value any other information which may be known to readers. Above all, he would be pleased to see any photographs, programmes and any other memorabilia of these theatres.

Theatre Royal – The original facade of the theatre 1856, not long after it was converted from a Racquets Court. Portsmouth City Archivist.

THEATRE ROYAL SOCIETY

– the Society which is helping one Portsmouth Theatre to come back to life!

The Theatre Royal Society is a 'supporters club', which seeks to help in the restoration and eventual day-to-day running of the Theatre Royal. So far, we have been instrumental in saving the building from demolition and in providing a volunteer labour force and some funds. We regularly show people around the Theatre, run a theatre shop, organize meetings, talks, social occasions, and visits to other theatres.

If you feel you could help in any way, or would just like to be a part of this exciting venture, WHY NOT JOIN THE THEATRE ROYAL SOCIETY? It will cost you just £2.00 per annum, and for that you will receive a regular newsletter containing details of all developments at the Theatre, and of forthcoming events.

Please send your first subscription, a cheque or postal order to the value of £2.00, made payable to the 'Theatre Royal Society' to:-

The Hon. Treasurer,
Theatre Royal Society,
New Theatre Royal,
White Swan Road, Portsmouth
Hampshire.

Acknowledgements

Appreciation is expressed to the following:-

First to Paul Smith, who spent many hours researching through past papers at the Central Library.

Elizabeth Duffy for reading the manuscript, and for correction of linguistic errors!

Eve Tipler for her original drawing of a Victorian audience.

Christopher Hyde Wear for his drawing of the façade of the "Coliseum that never was".

Laurie Upton for photographs and programmes of the Prince's Theatre.

K. Edmonds Gately for photographs of the South Parade Pier Theatre, the Portland Hall, and the drawing of the 1884 Theatre Royal.

Reverend Brother Lionel, F.S.C. for photographs of the Theatre Royal.

The City Archivist for providing a copy of a print of the Theatre Royal in High Street.

Messrs Holbrook & Sons Ltd for permission to publish extracts from the 'Portsmouth Times'; they were the publishers and printers of this excellent paper, which appeared between 1850 and 1926.

The Central Library for making available papers, posters and programmes, and for permission to reproduce some of them.

The Editor of 'The News', Portsmouth for allowing reproduction of articles and photographs.

For
Anton Stone
From Whom I Learnt
All I Know About
Theatre